LINDA & BLANCHE

Penrhyn to Festiniog

Blanche at Port Penrhyn, after bringing a slate train down from Bethesda on the Penrhyn Quarry Railway, 14th September 1960. *(Roger West)*

Dick Blenkinsop abp AB Publishing

Dick Blenkinsop comes from a family with legal connections and it is difficult to see where his love of the steam engine originated. Certainly this interest started early in life — in fact in the perambulator days and for many years the railway scene, with its profusion of locomotives, dominated his life.

A photographer, with a number of successful railway books covering the post-war period, he now looks at the narrow-gauge in this volume.

Holidays in North Wales provided the setting for the pictures of the Penrhyn Railway, and membership of the Festiniog Railway Preservation Society since 1960 has enabled his camera to capture *Linda* and *Blanche* over the subsequent years.

Front Cover. Blanche and *Linda* waiting at Boston Lodge just before departing to Harbour Station during the Centenary Gala Weekend. 2-5-93.

All rights reserved. No part of this book may be reproduced or transmitted in any form or by any means, electronic or mechanical, including photocopying, recording or by any information storage and retrieval system, without permission from the Publisher in writing.

© AB Publishing 1993

Printed in England by
AB Printers Limited
33 Cannock Street, Leicester LE4 7HR

ISBN 1-869915-05-4.

INTRODUCTION

The photographs in this book record a history and a celebration: the disappearance of a historic working railway, and the survival of some of its locomotives.

It was my good fortune to visit, on three occasions, the Penrhyn Quarry Railway while it was still in operation, though nearing the end of its life. In the summer of 1959 and 1960, we had our annual holiday at Abersoch, and, having a young family, I needed to earn 'Brownie Points' to be allowed one day off each year to visit the Padarn and the Penrhyn.

At this time too I came upon the Festiniog Railway, and at once joined the Preservation Society, as this was a project that required financial support, (and I am sure still does).

The main group of pictures are my work of many years ago, and it gives me great pleasure to have them published when *Linda* and *Blanche*, now at work on the Festiniog Railway, celebrate their centenary.

My last visit to the Penrhyn was in 1961, the year before closure, to take a ride on one of the empty slate wagons working back to the quarry. I remember walking in to Port House and asking if there was any chance of a member of the public being allowed to travel on the train. The answer was a prompt affirmative, though I had to sign a disclaimer form in case of an accident on the journey.

Linda shortly appeared with some empties and Dick Roberts the driver kindly provided a wooden plank which just fitted across the last wagon. Of course I had a camera with me, though not enough film to do full justice to the lovely countryside as we gently rattled up to the quarry at Coed-y-Parc. Thank goodness it was not raining.

My wife had managed to find her way to the quarry, and I well remember wondering, as we drove home, if it would be the last time I saw *Linda* at work.

I have twice returned to the railway recently to visit some of the sites where I took the original photographs, and it is amazing to see how things have changed over the years. Some of the track formation remains, but much is overgrown, so that in places it is not possible to believe that a railway existed.

'The Ladies' however, have fared much better than their track. They were bought by the Festiniog Railway in 1963, and have now been in use for 30 years at Porthmadog. It is good to see them still at work, complete with oil firing and the load they take up to Blaenau Ffestiniog. They were never worked as hard as this on the Penrhyn, so all the modifications made at Boston Lodge Works have enhanced their usefulness. *Blanche's* major overhaul was completed just in time for the Centenary Gala.

Putting these photographs together, and making a visit to North Wales for up-to-date views, has been a fascinating task. It felt quite strange to be using the same Leica Rangefinder camera that has been with me for over thirty years. Is that some sort of a record? Will today's cameras be with us in 2033? No doubt by then photography as we know it will not exist.

The 'Hunslet Hundred' Steam Gala, held on 1-3 May 1993, shows that some things do improve with age, as *Linda* and *Blanche* celebrated their centenary with a reunion with their 'elder brother' *Charles*, (preserved by the National Trust at Penrhyn Castle Museum and brought to Boston Lodge for the occasion).

Charles was on display outside Boston Lodge each day, while *Linda* and *Blanche* had two daily return workings to Blaenau Ffestiniog, usually carrying original large lamps, with a sand bucket on the leading engine, as in Penrhyn days. *Linda* sometimes had a full cab or, as shown in some pictures, the part attached to the tender was removed. Many other Hunslet locomotives were also present, but it is not possible to include them here.

I should like to thank all the hard-working people who made the weekend so memorable, and the staff of the Festiniog Railway, who went out of their way to make certain photographs possible.

A visit to the Festiniog Railway is always worthwhile and if you are interested in the Penrhyn Quarry Railway it is possible to walk along the track bed where it has been turned into a footpath. The Snowdon Mountain Railway and the Llanberis Lake Railway are also not far away.

ACKNOWLEDGEMENTS

I wish to express my gratitude to Rodney Weaver for his clear and concise contribution of the historical and technical background for this book; also to Norman Gurley, Frank Jones, Rodney Weaver and Roger West whose photographs so admirably supplement the efforts of the author. I must also thank the National Trust for allowing photography inside the Museum at Penrhyn Castle, and finally Colin Huston at AB Publishing who was responsible for the layout of the final publication.

Over the years the Penrhyn Quarry Railway has attracted much attention. The definitive work on the subject is *Narrow Gauge Railways in North Caernarvonshire Volume 2*, 'The Penrhyn Quarry Railway' by James I.C. Boyd, published by Oakwood Press. This splendid book covers the history of the line from the early days with details of all the locomotives and rolling stock, and gives a real insight into the operation of the Slate Industry in North Wales.

THE NUMBERED PHOTOGRAPHS WERE TAKEN AT THE POINTS SHOWN BELOW

PENRHYN QUARRY RAILWAY

Penrhyn Railway ▬▬▬▬
L.M.S. Railway ▬▬▬▬

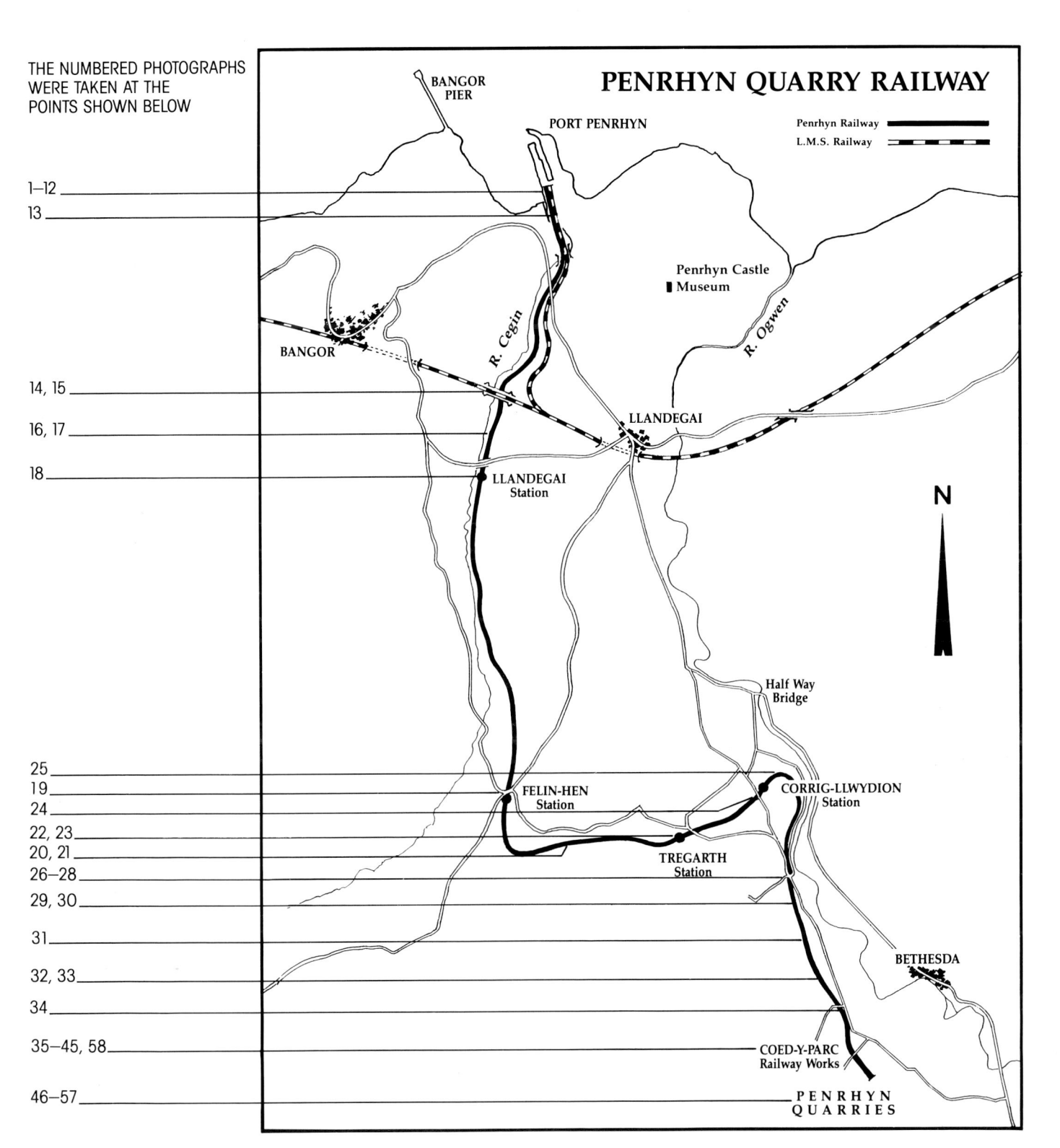

- 1–12
- 13
- 14, 15
- 16, 17
- 18
- 25
- 19
- 24
- 22, 23
- 20, 21
- 26–28
- 29, 30
- 31
- 32, 33
- 34
- 35–45, 58
- 46–57

Locations shown on map: BANGOR PIER, PORT PENRHYN, Penrhyn Castle Museum, R. Cegin, R. Ogwen, BANGOR, LLANDEGAI, LLANDEGAI Station, Half Way Bridge, FELIN-HEN Station, CORRIG-LLWYDION Station, TREGARTH Station, BETHESDA, COED-Y-PARC Railway Works, PENRHYN QUARRIES

The first Hunslet locomotive supplied to the Penrhyn Railway was *Charles* in 1882. Shown on main line duty at Coed-y-Parc in May 1951 *(Frank Jones photo)* in May 1963 it was placed on permanent display at Penrhyn Castle Museum.

3

THE PENRHYN RAILWAY

Blanche gleaming in the late afternoon sunlight at Port Penrhyn on 14th September 1960 *(Roger West)*

HISTORICAL & TECHNICAL BACKGROUND

LINDA and *BLANCHE* are surely the best purchase the Festiniog Railway has ever made. Sixty-nine years old when they arrived, they quickly established themselves as preferred motive power for all but the heaviest trains and at the beginning of their centennial year had been responsible for more than one third of the total locomotive mileage run since restoration began in 1954.

They were built by the Hunslet Engine Company of Leeds for the 'main line' of the Penrhyn Railway, the principal outlet from the vast Penrhyn Quarry above Bethesda, about six miles south east of Bangor. Down this private railway passed slate for onward carriage from Port Penrhyn by ship or main line railway, coal and other quarry supplies being taken uphill together with the empty slate wagons. Penrhyn was the first quarry to enjoy direct rail access to the coast, a horse-worked tramroad being constructed in 1801 and replaced by a steam-operated railway in 1879; the Festiniog Railway too was originally a slate railway, built in 1832-36 to serve the quarries at Blaenau Ffestiniog and upgraded to a steam-hauled *public* railway in 1863-65.

Hunslet supplied many locomotives to the slate industry, most of them for use on internal quarry railways, but 'The Ladies' are rather different in concept. The first 'main line' locomotives on the Penrhyn Railway were built by the local firm of de Winton & Company, Caernarfon, better known for their simple, vertical boiler quarry locomotives whose popularity rivalled that of the more conventional Hunslet product, but their first attempt at something more elaborate was none too successful and as early as 1882 Lord Penrhyn ordered a replacement from Hunslet. This locomotive *Charles*, was built at the same time as a pair of locomotives for the Darjeeling Himalayan Railway sub-contracted from Sharp Stewart & Company of Manchester and when seen in silhouette is reminiscent of a Darjeeling locomotive. This may of course be coincidental, but the two railways had similar characteristics in all save one respect — the Darjeeling was steeper.

The subjects of this book are slightly enlarged versions of *Charles* which replaced the remaining pair of horizontally boilered de Wintons. Works number 589 *Blanche* was completed on 22 July 1893 and 590 *Linda* a week later. Like *Charles* they were named after members of the Penrhyn family and for the next sixty-odd years this trio effectively monopolised main line working on the Penrhyn Railway. They worked between Port Penrhyn and sidings just inside the quarry, from which an incline led up to quarry proper, a distance of just over six miles climbing 550ft on an average gradient of 1 in 62 with three miles at 1 in 40 and a short stretch of 1 in 33. Reliability rather than all-out performance was required, the maximum train weight being 40-45 tons (sixty empty slate wagons or their equivalent) and the journey time of one hour requiring nothing faster than 8-10 mph.

The Penrhyn Railway remained busy until the mid-1950s, after which traffic declined rapidly with the disappearance of coastal shipping and the shift from rail to road for inland carriage. By 1962 the railway had become uneconomic; on 28 June 1962 *Blanche* hauled the last steam-worked slate train and it was announced that the line would close on 24 July, diesel locomotives being able to handle the remaining traffic.

Continued on page 45

1 — It must be 'Lunch Break Time' for the BR crew who have come down the branch from the Holyhead main line and are sitting in the sun at Port Penrhyn. The 3F 0-6-0 No 47558 was shedded at Bangor (6H). On the left are the narrow gauge sidings and the coal stacks for the locomotives, and on the right the narrow gauge line to the locomotive shed and the chain supports to the flagpole. The scene today is very much into the leisure industry with boats parked in all directions and the silver birch trees doing very well. 12-6-59.

2 — This gives a good view of Port Penrhyn with, in the background, the River Menai and the wooded shores of Anglesey. To the left is the old weighbridge and to the right of the last wagon can be seen the circular lavatory for the use of the slate loaders and now out of use!

The second unit of the train is a brake van made in the quarry workshops from the remains of the locomotive *Sanford*, originally built by W.G. Bagnall Ltd. Note the new sand bucket hanging on the smokebox door as *Blanche* moves off with the empties for the quarry.

3 — I have included this photograph of the point work as it shows the stub movement in the foreground and the switchblade 'Frog', both operated by one lever through the point rodding on the right. 10-6-60.

4

4 — My 1957 Morris Minor is on the left of the photograph as the BR train with a small load departs for the climb up to the main line and then no doubt a short trip into Bangor. Port House, the administrative offices of the Penrhyn Quarry Railway, stands out well and is still in use together with the small building on the right, but the trees in the centre have grown well in 31 years. 29-9-61.

5 — Perhaps this is unique? The narrow gauge crosses the standard gauge tracks and used to enable the narrow gauge locomotives to get to and from the shed each morning and evening. The narrow gauge track is operated by one rod to swivel the rails so that they move onto the steel plates just inside the bull head track and provide clearance for the wheels of the standard gauge locomotive and wagons. 10-6-60.

6 — At the end of a working day *Blanche* crosses the standard gauge track on her way to the locomotive shed. I am not sure if that is a young man hoping to be a driver one day and looking out of the cab but quite often there was a teenager riding the locomotive. 10-6-60.

9

7 — A good close up of *Linda* just before my ride up to the quarry in the empty slate wagon at the end of the train. It is good to see how well the engine was looked after in a perfect state of cleanliness and all the internal and external brass work polished. The first three wagons contain coal for the quarry engines and note the wooden frame. In the background is Port House. 29-9-61.

8 — I have included these two photographs as they show so clearly how Port Penrhyn has changed since the railway was closed. Hundreds of people must go down here each year and I am sure they have no idea that a railway ever existed which took slate to all parts of the world. 10-6-60.

9 — Turning round from the previous picture is the view looking south showing the standard gauge and narrow gauge tracks leaving the Harbour complex. The line to the right used to go to the coal wharfs as most of the coal came in from The Point of Ayre Colliery by sea. 10-6-60.

10 — Now *Blanche* is getting into her stride and just about to pass under Port Bridge. The changed scene today is quite dramatic as I assume the two arches have become lock-up garages and the creeper has made itself felt all over the stonework. 10-6-60.

11 — Watering of the locomotives took place under Port bridge and here *Linda* is having the tank topped up before leaving for the quarry. In today's scene the arch has been bricked up but the remains of one of the gates hangs forlornly on its hinges. 12-6-59.

12 — The last of the photographs taken at Port Penrhyn as *Linda* leaves after the water stop. The semaphore signal informed drivers of northbound trains how the mixed-gauge crossing was set as shown on a previous photograph. 12-6-59.

13

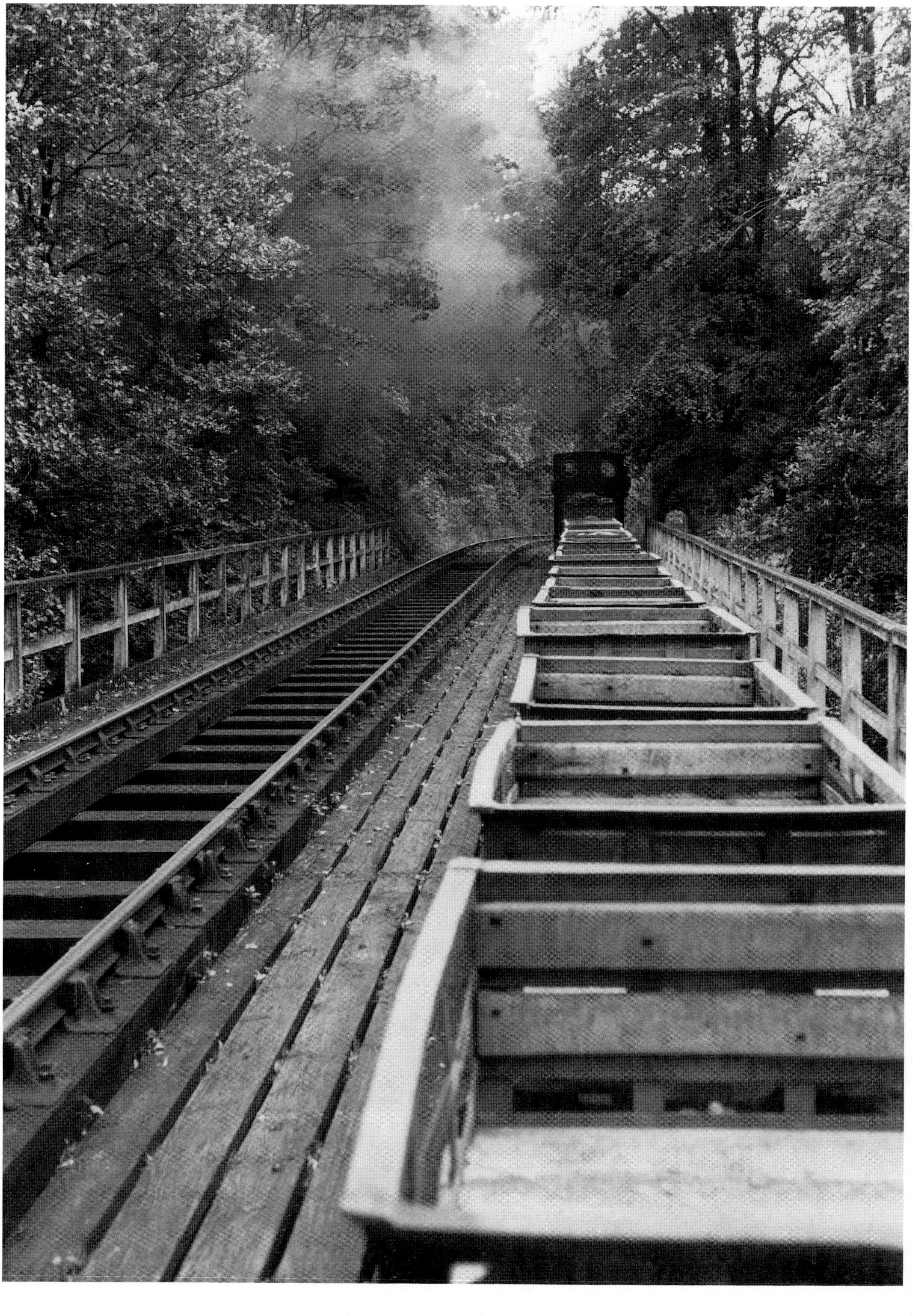

13 — The view from the last wagon of the train on which I travelled from Port Penrhyn to Coed-y-Parc not many months before closure. The bridge carries the line and the standard gauge over the River Cegin; this is the first of two crossings of the river very soon after leaving Port Penrhyn and also one of the steepest gradients on the line. 29-9-61.

14 — A view of the fine stone viaduct which carries the North Wales main line over the Cegin Valley and also the Penrhyn Quarry Railway. As can be seen from the present day photograph the trackbed has been turned into the most delightful walk heading south from where the A5122 crosses the line as it enters Bangor. 29-9-61.

15

15 — Just a hundred yards further on the train passed under the viaduct. Note the way in which the trees and hedges have grown over the years, but steam still passes from time to time with the main line specials from Crewe to Holyhead. 29-9-61.

16 — It is not easy or sometimes possible to find exactly the same place where I had taken the main photograph. *Linda* has a very short train of empties on this glorious summer's day with the second man living rather dangerously off the side of the cab. 12-6-59.

17 — As the train goes by another view shows the condition of the track and the approach to the White Bridge which carries a minor road down from Llandegai. 12-6-59.

18 — The south side of the White Bridge is shown here with *Blanche* working quite hard in the most delightful scenery. Just to the left the road drops down to a ford where the clear Cegin bubbles its way down the valley and provided me with a good place, in 1992, for a sleep after lunch. 10-6-60.

19

19 — A quick dash in the car from the previous photograph up the side roads brought me to Felin-Hen where the line crossed the present B4366 and, as can be compared with today's scene, the road layout has been dramatically altered.

The only give away in the modern photograph is the stone wall which supported the end of the bridge. Dick Roberts the driver is just about to give a wave as *Blanche* runs on to the next embankment. 10-6-60.

20 — So we come to the only passing loop on the Penrhyn Quarry Railway and for some unknown reason we made a stop. This is just before Tregarth which can be seen in the background, also on the extreme left the road bridge which crosses the LNWR branch to Bethesda. The late Norman Lockett leans against the fence while the late Ivo Peters records the scene with his cine camera. 29-9-61.

21 — The train is now leaving the passing loop and the other line is just visible to the right of the picture. Note the way the metal fencing has been pushed over by the cattle and the trackbed is now a field for horse grazing. 29-9-61.

22 — *Blanche* passes under the bridge which carries the main road through the village of Tregarth. The cutting in the background is now filled in and part of a garden. It also looks as if the bridge was demolished and a new wall constructed and it is now a meeting place for the children after school. 10-6-60.

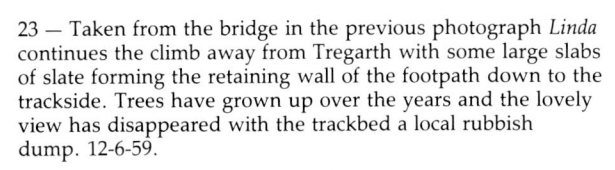

23 — Taken from the bridge in the previous photograph *Linda* continues the climb away from Tregarth with some large slabs of slate forming the retaining wall of the footpath down to the trackside. Trees have grown up over the years and the lovely view has disappeared with the trackbed a local rubbish dump. 12-6-59.

24 — The skew bridge survives today just visible through the trees from a minor road outside Tregarth. *Blanche* is running back to Port Penrhyn in the afternoon with the loaded train and is seen here crossing the branch to Bethesda which is in a deep rock cutting and a hundred yards before plunging into Dinas Tunnel. 10-6-60.

25 — For the last mile or so the line has been in a west east direction but now it turns south round the edge of a hill on a very sharp curve with lovely views to the north. 29-9-61.

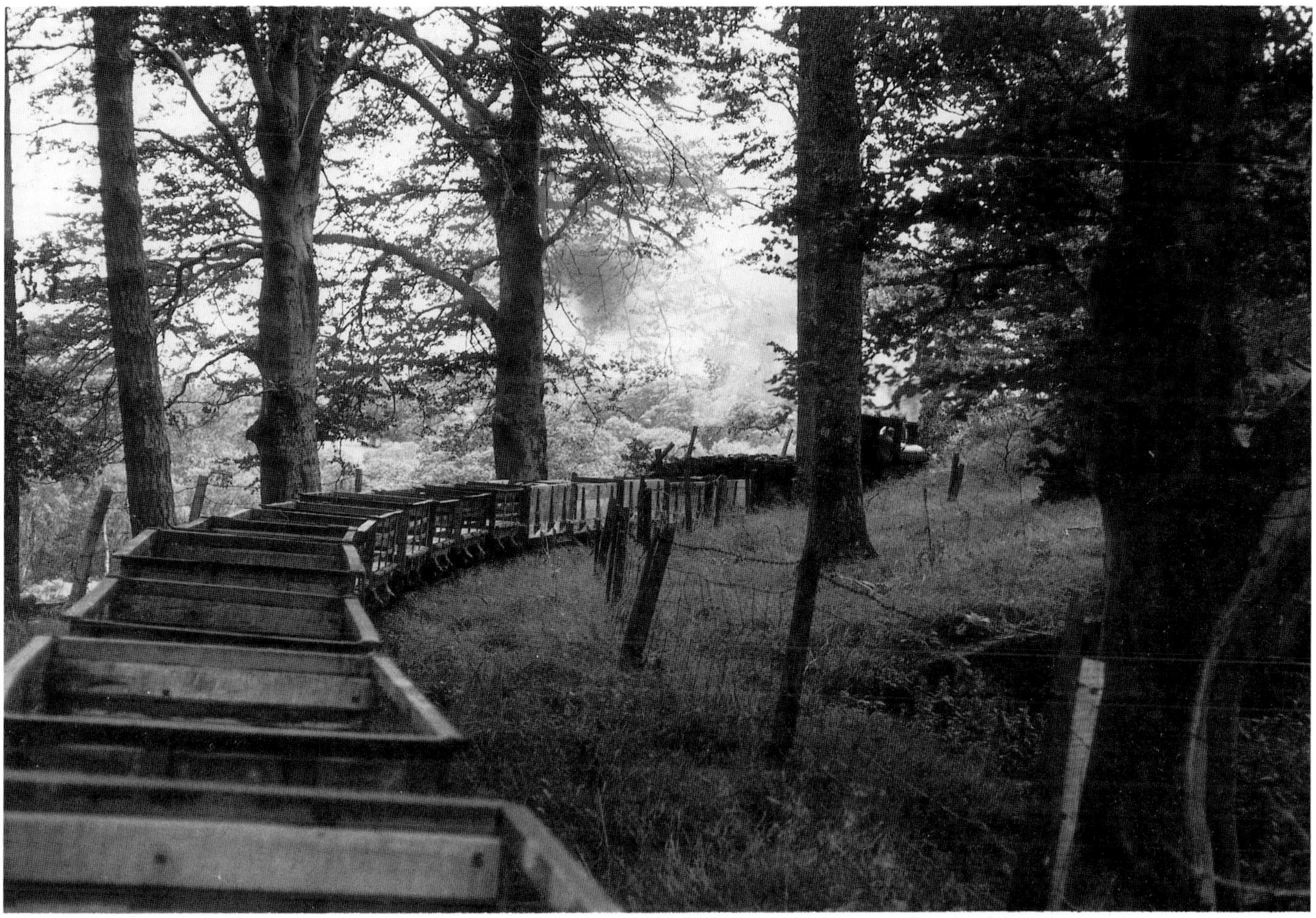

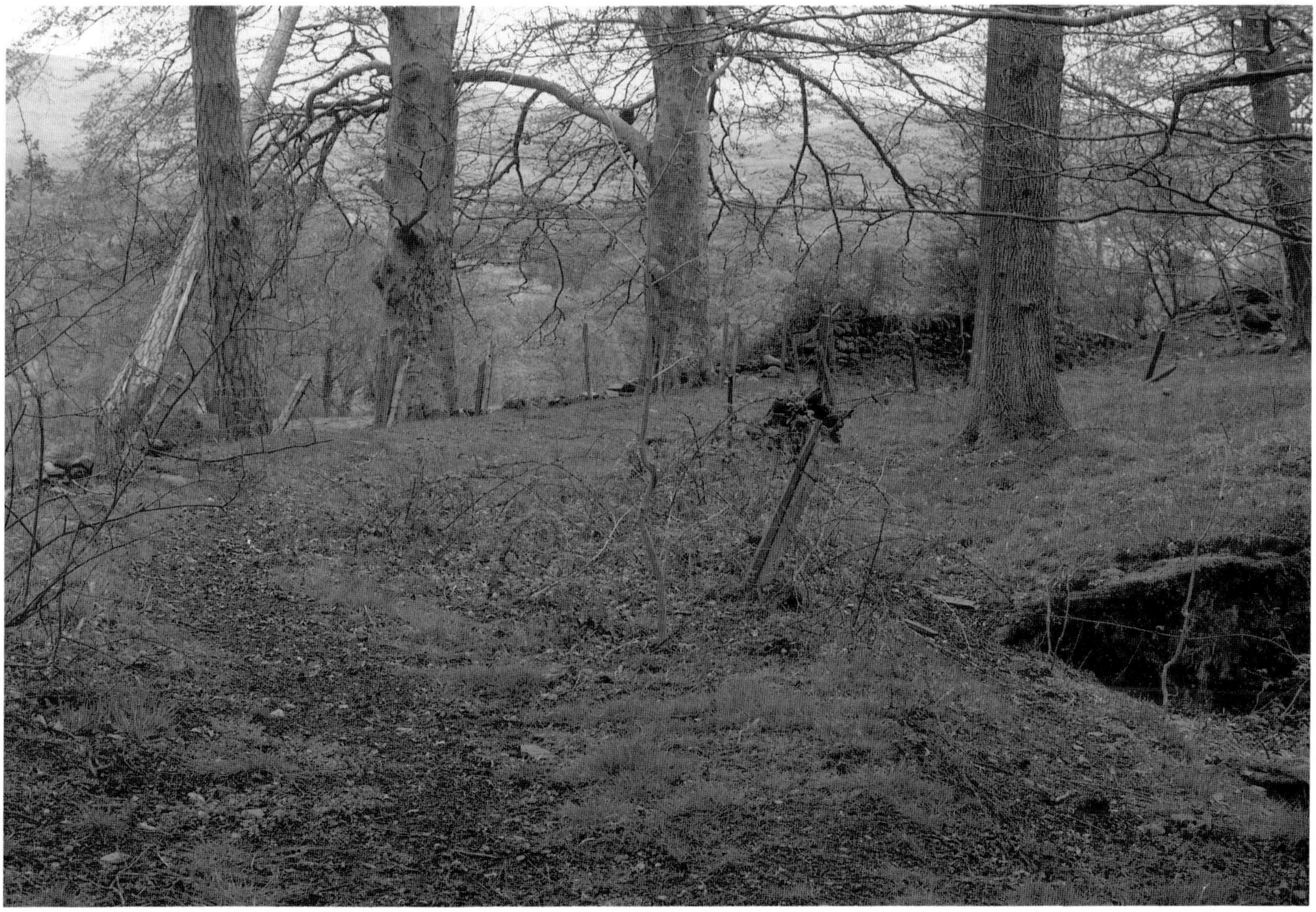

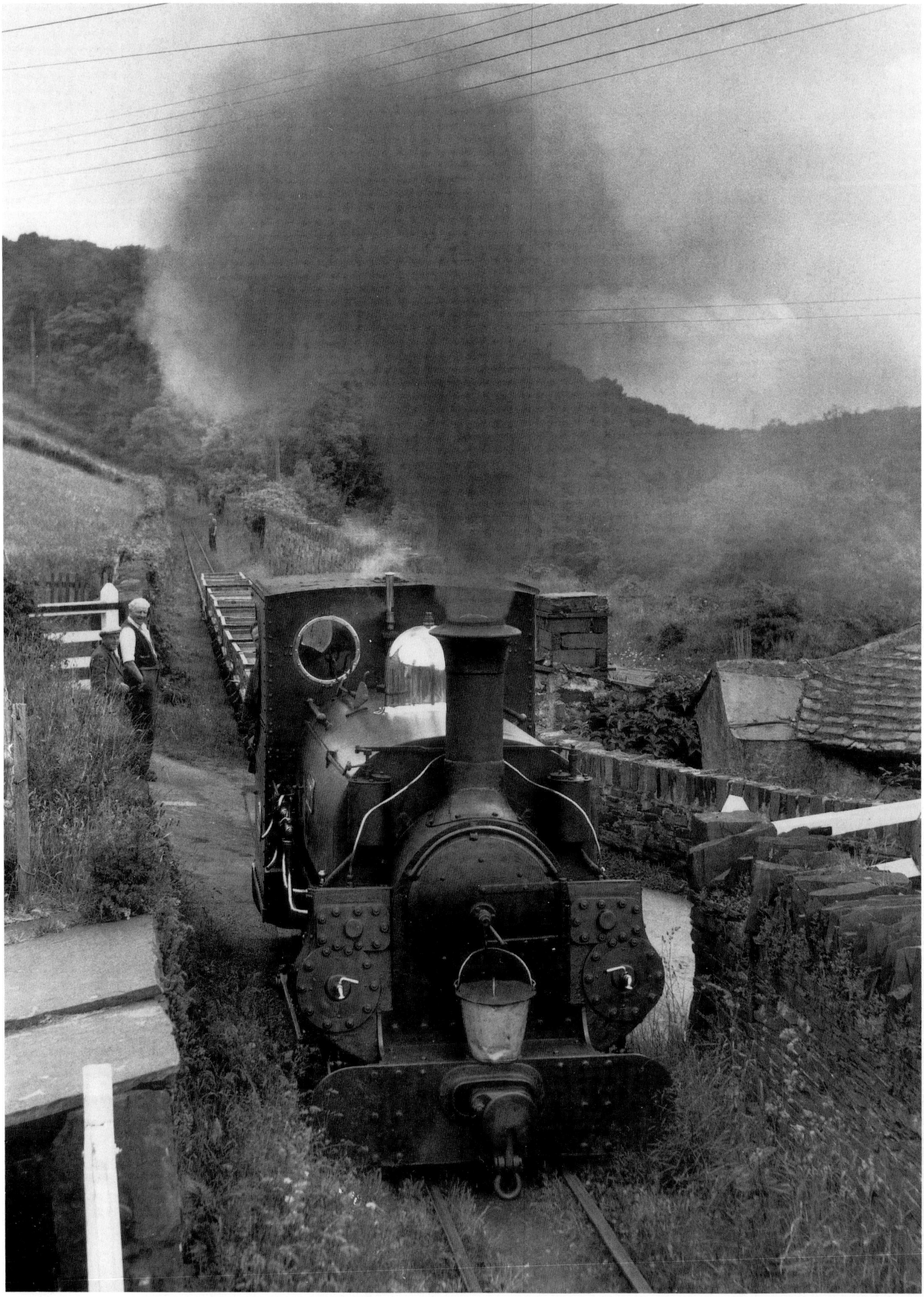

26

26 — The crossing keeper Mr Hughes looks after the level-crossing at Hen-Durnpike while I take my photograph from inside his hut, now a garden shed for the house on the hill. The road has been rebuilt and carries quite a lot of traffic from Tregarth to Bethesda. 12-6.59.

27 — The same location showing the signal which was used to inform the driver that the road gates had been closed. The trackbed is now used for access to the houses. 29-9-61.

28 — These two photographs show the signal in operation even though the gates are closed, also the substantial nature of the track. I expect it was quite warm in the hut during the winter with the stove in action. 10-6-60.

29 — This was an occasion when *Linda* was steaming badly, so having taken this photograph at the back of the houses at Bron-Ogwen I managed to scramble down to the trackside and run in front of the train to the next location. 12-6-59.

30 — Just a little further on this view gives a good idea of the gorgeous countryside through which the railway ran. Would it have been good as a preservation project? 12-6-59.

31 — This is my favourite photograph on the Penrhyn Quarry Railway. Having dashed up the line in front of the train I came to this delightful setting with the trees forming an arch over the track. Note the slate fencing which was almost universal along the line. 12-6-59.

32

32 — As the train approaches the end of its journey on a slate embankment there is a view of Bethesda Station in the distance and the village lying in the valley. Here the railway crosses a footpath and the view today is somewhat different. 10-6-60.

33 — *Linda* crosses the road bridge at Cilgeraint through a slate cutting serving both the railway and the road. As can be seen in the modern picture all has recently been cleared away complete with the old road sign. 12-6-59.

34 — *Blanche* returning to Port Penrhyn in the afternoon with a loaded slate train at the same location as the previous shot. The shape of the frames can easily be seen, and the large overhang on each side of the wheels. 10-6-60.

31

35

36

32

37 — Dick Roberts the driver of *Blanche* fills up the tank and poses for his photograph. A kind man, he was always so pleased to help with placing the engines where I wanted them to get the best picture. 10-6-60.

38 — After watering *Blanche* takes a rest before the shunting operation takes place when the crew have returned from having a cup of tea. The desolation of the years from closure is now being put right with an industrial enterprise using some of the buildings. 10-6-60.

35 — The train arriving at Coed-y-Parc with a line of withdrawn locomotives on the left beside one of the Slab Mills. In the distance can be seen the quarry workings and the enormous slate tip. 29-9-61.

36 — This is the end of my journey riding in the slate wagon. The train has stopped at the water column seen behind *Linda's* chimney. The works complex is to the right and out of the picture. 29-9-61.

39 — The gated overbridge to the south of the Coed-y-Parc complex frames *Blanche* as she shunts the brake van to one side before pulling the slate wagons forward into the marshalling yards. Today the access has been filled with blocks of slate and stone blocking the entrance. 10-6-60.

40 & 41 — *Blanche* coupled up to a loaded slate train shortly to leave for the return journey to Port Penrhyn. Note the slabs of slate on the other wagons waiting to go down to the slab mill. Trees cover the site today. 10-6-60.

35

42

43

42 — This is the view from the front door of the workshop with *Nesta* having some work done on the smokebox and *Blanche* in the background. Note the lineshaft for driving the machine tools. 12-6-59.

43 — Hunslet *Gertrude* on the left with *Ogwen* and *Linda*. 10-6-60.

44 — *Blanche* looks as if she is ready for the road and *Cegin* or *Glyder* is having a major overhaul with the boiler off and attention being given to the motion work. Note the well tank type of construction and the water filler — a tidy and clean workshop. 29-9-61.

45 — The empty workshop as it is today.

46 & 47 — Whilst this book is devoted to the three main line Hunslet locomotives I felt I could not miss the opportunity to include a selection of the quarry engines still working on my first visit in 1959. These two pictures on a rather stormy day show *Cegin* at rest in the sun and also with a short train. Both *Cegin* and *Glyder* were second-hand engines to the quarry and made by A. Barclay Sons & Co Ltd. 12-6-59.

46

47

38

48 & 49 — Both *Ogwen* and *Marchlyn* were built by The Avonside Engine Co Ltd and again were purchased by the quarry second-hand. In fact all the four engines mentioned came from The Durham County Water Board shortly before the second world war. Note the weather protection round the cab. 12-6-59.

50

50, 51, 52, 53 & 54 — On one of the top levels of the quarry *Glyder* is shown outside its shed during the lunch break and then pulling a train of slate to go to the slate mills. In front another load of slate which may be tipped over the edge of the mountain. The last picture gives a good idea how deep is the quarry with a train making its way to the workings on the right of the picture. 12-6-59.

41

53

54

55, 56, 57 — *Winifred* was one of the Port Class engines and spent most of its life down at Port Penrhyn shunting the trains brought in by *Charles*, *Linda* and *Blanche*. Here she is on the top level with a close-up of the footplate. Built in 1885 by The Hunslet Engine Co Ltd she was finally sold to America in 1965. Note the steam navvy in the background and the bare landscape. 12-6-59.

58 — For the last photograph I have chosen *Linda* leaving Coed-y-Parc for the journey back to Port Penrhyn with loaded slate wagons. The track leading off to the right goes into the locomotive workshop on a very sharp curve and it looks as if two of the wagons have the brakes pinned down for the downhill journey.

THE FESTINIOG RAILWAY

The final years of the Penrhyn Railway coincided with the revival of the Festiniog Railway and July 1962 found the latter with a locomotive crisis on its hands. Without more ado *Linda* was hired for the rest of the season as spare engine, making a trial trip on the evening of 14 July. She worked several turns before derailing rather spectacularly on 5 September, whereupon she was withdrawn pending certain essential modifications like regauging from 1ft 10¾in to 1ft 11½in and improving stability at the higher running speed of FR trains. By agreement with her owners, sufficient work was done to permit a return to service for the 1963 summer timetable for extended assessment. Liking what they saw, the FR purchased both locomotives, *Blanche* arriving on 17 December. (*Charles* — long unserviceable — was later placed in Penrhyn Castle Museum and was reunited with *Linda* and *Blanche* during the May 1993 'Hunslet Hundred' Gala in celebration of their centenary.)

This is a convenient point at which to describe the locomotives as running on their original line before tracing subsequent developments in FR ownership. They were 0-4-0 saddle tanks with outside plate frames and outside cylinders inclined at 1 in 6 so that the connecting rod works inside the coupling rods, whereby the cylinders can be brought closer together to reduce the width of the locomotive. The cylinders were of 10½in bore × 12in stroke with slide valves on top driven by a rocking shaft from Stephenson valve gear mounted between the frames. Overall length was approximately 17ft but the coupled wheelbase only 5ft, the driving wheels being 2ft 1in nominal diameter, and they weighed 12 tons 6cwt in working order (10 tons 10cwt empty). The boiler had a raised-top firebox casing wider than the barrel, containing a deep, square inner box with 5.2sq.ft grate area; the 28in diameter barrel contained sixty-six firetubes of 1¾in outside diameter, 9ft long. Total fire-side heating surface, including firebox, was 259sq.ft and the working pressure 140lb/sq.in. Nominal tractive effort, based on 85% of boiler pressure, was 6300lb giving a minimum adhesive factor (bunker empty, tank one third full) of almost exactly 4, rather low for something that would do a lot of hard work in the notoriously wet climate of North Wales.

The locomotives were fitted with a saddle tank containing 270 gallons of water and a coal bunker of 12cu.ft (about 6cwt) capacity inside the cab. They were driven from the right-hand side of the footplate and as was then customary the two injectors were on the driver's side, mounted below the saddle tank. Braking

Linda is given a first test run after her arrival at the Festiniog Railway on 15 July 1962.
(Alan Garraway)

Blanche leaving Coed-y-Parc on 17 December 1963 bound for a new lease of service life.
(Alan Garraway)

was by means of a screw handbrake and although sandboxes were fitted ahead of the tank (dropping sand in front of the leading wheels) the usual practice was to carry a bucket of sand hung on the smokebox door, the fireman getting off and sanding by hand when necessary.

The livery was lined black, closely resembling the black livery of the London & North Western Railway introduced in 1874.

To suit FR requirements the locomotives were regauged, converted to left-hand drive, equipped with vacuum brake

Departing from Minffordd in the afternoon *Linda* sets out for the next stop at Penrhyn. What a lovely setting with the trees and the summer sun adding to the picture. July 1964.

equipment and provided with tenders carrying rather more than a ton of coal and an extra 150 gallons of water. A graduable steam brake was installed on the engine, this being operated either by its own lever or automatically by the vacuum brake. One of the original injectors was removed and replaced by a more modern one mounted under the cab and taking water either from the tank or from the tender. *Linda*, whose first regular driver was FR General Manager Allan Garraway, retained her open-backed cab but *Blanche* was provided with a tender cab giving a longer and less exposed footplate. Both locomotives were painted standard FR green. In deference to the overhanging weight at either end of the engines, their new tenders were attached by a load-bearing drawbar to act as stabilisers. Thus modified they proved excellent machines, powerful enough to handle eight coaches if required, free steaming and only rarely giving their crews an anxious few seconds by starting to dance.

By 1968 *Linda* required a certain amount of attention to her boiler and the opportunity was taken to install a superheater; at the same time the boiler pressure was raised to 160lb/sq.in on both locomotives — raising the nominal tractive effort to 7200lb at the expense of an adhesive factor of 3.5. It made them a little less sure-footed in the wet but this was outweighed by the increased economy that resulted from using a shorter cut-off and consequently greater degree of expansion. While stripped down, *Linda* was provided with a pony truck to stabilise the front end, becoming a 2-4-0.

On 2 November 1970 *Linda* emerged from Boston Lodge equipped with a Laidlaw Drew oil burner, taking an empty five-car train to Tan y bwlch and back. The conversion was relatively simple and did not preclude a return to coal at short notice, being inspired by the spiralling cost of fire insurance and fire patrols and the (then) favourable price of oil. The grate was replaced by a plate through which passed a number of inclined air tubes and the lower part of the firebox lined with a firebrick to prevent erosion and overheating of the plates at burner level. The steam atomising burner was mounted in the centre of the swirl plate, steam being employed to produce a conical spray of finely divided oil which burnt in the turbulent air emerging from the air tubes; the locomotive was lit up using compressed air. Heat output was controlled by regulating oil feed and adjusting the atomising pressure, induced draught being required whenever the oil was alight.

As first installed it proved impossible to match the performance of a coal-fired locomotive but by modifying the burner to pass more oil and produce a near horizontal spray pattern and increasing the number of air tubes *Linda* was soon performing as well as she had ever done on coal, cleaner (albeit noisier) and more predictable. The oil tanks were installed in the tender, occupying the coal space, and this added to the confusion of those to whom a steam locomotive automatically burnt coal.

With *Linda* performing satisfactorily the rest of the fleet were converted as quickly as possible, after which *Blanche* was converted to a superheated 2-4-0 and given new cylinders with outside-admission piston valves. The new cylinders were fabricated instead of being cast and distorted slightly in service; the change was made not to improve cylinder efficiency but to reduce the load on the valve gear and was not considered worth extending to *Linda* even though a second pair of cylinders had been made.

During front-end modifications a strange weakness in the original Hunslet design came to light: the cylinders were attached to the frames only by one row of bolts, the upper mounting flange being bolted to the smokebox. New front ends

Leaving Tan-y-bwlch for the downhill run to Porthmadog and a light load of five carriages. At this time *Linda* was still coal fired and the supply in the tender looks alarmingly low! July 1964.

47

were therefore fabricated in which the bottom half of the smokebox is integral with the frames to support the cylinders properly; the box being thus split horizontally the top is removable giving unobstructed access to the pipework within.

An amusing aside on the conversion to oil concerns smokebox paint, for the smokebox temperature was much higher than was normally the case when burning coal. The black originally used could not withstand the increased temperature and after several fruitless enquiries for a better black paint the smokeboxes were reluctantly painted aluminium; nobody liked it, but the alternative was authentic rust colour. A visitor to the Puffing Billy line in Australia discovered that they had found a local supply of heat-resistant black; further enquiries disclosed that the paint was imported from Britain — it was in fact made at Bethesda within sight of the Penrhyn Quarries!

Having converted to oil, the FR now found that the price of oil had increased dramatically and was forced to investigate the use of waste oil. This was cheaper but of variable quality and did not burn cleanly: with gas oil one could maintain a faint haze at the top of the chimney but now absence of smoke meant absence of steam. The oil could be very dirty, too: *Linda* once completed an Up journey 1½ hours late as a woodburner, after which a centrifuge was obtained to improve cleanliness. The use of waste oil was eventually discontinued because of its variable and unknown composition.

Linda was the subject of a more formal experiment with alternative fuel in 1985 when she was converted to the gas producer system developed by Porta and Chapelon. This is capable of burning small, low grade and hence cheap coal otherwise unsuitable for locomotives. Only a limited amount of air, mixed with steam, is admitted below the fire which therefore generates carburetted water gas. This is burnt in air admitted above the fire, producing a very hot and clean fireball. It is a very responsive system and the decision not to pursue the matter was no reflection upon *Linda's* performance in service. She retains the Lempor exhaust system installed as part of the conversion, giving her a much sharper exhaust note than other FR locomotives.

The conversion coincided with *Linda's* first general overhaul since 1970, in which interval she had covered approximately 112,000 miles, a remarkable achievement for the average British standard gauge locomotive, let alone a narrow gauge machine approaching its centenary. To the dedicated locomotive enthusiast, this is something that sets the FR apart from most of its contemporaries, for its locomotives really work for a living and amass high annual mileages as they would have done in the heyday of the slate industry. FR steam locomotives frequently exceed 10,000 miles in a year, the highest on record being 12,500 as long ago as 1972. Compared with the demands of the Penrhyn Railway, *Linda* and *Blanche* are actually working harder than they used to do, being now expected to haul trains weighing 60-65 tons over long stretches of curving 1 in 80 gradient at 18-20 mph.

By the end of 1992 *Linda* had run 196,303 miles in FR ownership and *Blanche* (undergoing a protracted general overhaul) 183,101 miles. Their combined total of 379,404 represented 36% of the 1,041,000 locomotive miles run since the line reopened in 1955.

Near milepost 7 and Whistling Curve *Linda* heads for Tan-y-bwlch half a mile further on with Alan Garraway driving. July 1964.

Above: Within a few hours of arriving on the FR from the Penrhyn Quarry Railway in August 1962, *Linda* was at work collecting loaded coal wagons from Minffordd exchange sidings.
(Norman Gurley)

Linda and *Prince* leave Minffordd for Tan-y-bwlch in late August 1962.
(Norman Gurley)

Fitted with tender and vacuum brake, *Linda* leaves Harbour Station Porthmadog in August 1963.

Newly painted and with custom-built tender, *Linda* poses on Bryn Mawr for a Wales Tourist Board photographer in June 1964.
(Norman Gurley)

49

In 1964 the terminus was at Tan-y-bwlch and *Linda* is seen taking on water before running round the train for the return journey. July 1964.

Taken from the A496 road bridge and just opposite the site of the old LNWR station *Linda* nears the end of the journey with the 12.45 departure from Porthmadog. 28-4-92.

Crossing the road at Glan-y-pwll *Linda* makes for the terminus at Blaenau Ffestiniog. The scene gives a good idea of the slate terrain through which the railway passes. 26-4-92.

51

About to reverse into Harbour Station *Linda* in immaculate green livery stands in front of the now demolished Brittania Foundry.
August 1964.

In temporary black livery, *Blanche* prepares to leave Minffordd yard with a permanent way materials train during the three weeks in September 1965 when units from 16 Railway Regiment, Longmoor, were operating the FR as a training exercise.
(Norman Gurley)

Linda and *Blanche* side by side in 1964 at Harbour Station, before *Blanche* was fitted with the new piston valve cylinders. *(Rodney Weaver)*

Linda at the east end of the Cob and about to pass Boston Lodge Works. Note the road traffic in the background below the railway. September 1968. *(Rodney Weaver)*

Linda stands just below Garnedd Tunnel with an evening cine-photographers' special in July 1966. The new 'Centenary' coaches were much too large to pass through the tunnel before it was enlarged the following year. *(Norman Gurley)*

In coal firing days both the 'Ladies' are shown in the yard at Boston Lodge. August 1968.

Below: *Linda* has just passed through Garnedd Tunnel and will shortly stop at Tan-y-bwlch station. August 1968.

53

'Oiling up' at Tan-y-bwlch with attention being given to the Crosshead Slippers. Note the modern mechanical lubricator, a far cry from the days of the Penrhyn Quarry Railway. 25-4-92.

With the first train of the day *Linda* arrives at Minffordd, moving slowly up the platform. 25-4-92.

Blanche waits with an up train while the signalman exchanges tokens with *Linda*'s fireman on the down train, which won't need to stop at Rhiw Goch passing loop. September 1977. *(Norman Gurley)*

Below: *Blanche* coasts into Tan-y-bwlch in June 1978. *(Norman Gurley)*

Linda's footplate showing the various controls and the enormous amount of polishing these required on a daily basis. October 1977.

Pulling away from Penrhyn Station *Linda* will be soon slowing for Penrhyn Crossing just off to the right of the picture. May 1992.
Linda assists *Earl of Merioneth* with a heavy train on 5 May 1990. *(Norman Gurley)*

THE CENTENARY GALA

With Dduallt Station in the left background *Blanche* and *Linda* climb the spiral and have just crossed over Rhoslyn Bridge with the 13.45 up train from Porthmadog. Paul Martin looks out of the cab. 1-5-93.

A peaceful scene in Boston Lodge Yard the day before the Centenary Gala started. *Dafydd Lloyd George*, *Holy War* and *Charles* will soon be surrounded by visitors. 30-4-93.

For the last time *Charles, Blanche* and *Linda* stand in the sun outside Boston Lodge before the two ladies depart for the day's work. 3-5-93.

Tanygrisiau Station is just off the picture to the right and *Blanche* and *Linda* pull away with the 12.00 down train from Blaenau Ffestiniog. 1-5-93.

The sun is head on for the line up around 09.30 each morning so making black shadows down the side of the engines. *Prince* may be seen behind *Charles* being used to position the engine in exactly the right place. 3-5-93.

On the Saturday evening a Birthday Party was held for the two ladies in Minffordd Yard and here they are in the late evening sunshine being toasted by the assembled company. On the front of *Blanche* hangs a birthday card and fairy lights from the chimney to the cab. 1-5-93.

Nearing the end of the journey with the 10.45 up from Porthmadog, *Blanche* and *Linda* run alongside the River Barlwyd shortly before milepost 13. 3-5-93.

The sun has just gone behind the clouds as *Linda* and *Blanche* have emerged from Moelwyn Tunnel seen in the right background with Archer Dam visible above the last coach. The working is the 13.45 up from Porthmadog on 3rd May 1993.

The A4085 from Beddgelert to Penrhyn crosses the line at a level crossing which has to be staffed when the trains are running. Here *Blanche* comes across the road just after stopping at Penrhyn Station. 30-4-93.

Palmerston and *Dafydd Lloyd George* cross the Cob with the 09.30 from Harbour Station with the morning mixed train, the slate wagons being at the rear. *Blanche* and *Linda* are waiting to run tender first to Porthmadog. 3-5-93.

A slightly off beat photograph, but I could not resist the large American car standing by the line at Milepost 13. A lucky flash of sunshine appears as *Linda* and *Blanche* pass with the 12.00 down from Blaenau Ffestiniog. 3-5-93.

Taken outside Boston Lodge these show some of the changes that have taken place over the years between a pure Penrhyn locomotive and the rebuilt *Linda*. Top 30-4-93, bottom 28.4.92.

63

This threequarter front view ot *Charles* provides details of the livery carried by the Penrhyn engines. 30-4-93.

Charles with sand bucket on the buffer beam has the company of *Holy War* and *Dafydd Lloyd George* at Boston Lodge. 30-4-93.

64